Tongue Action

"There's Power In Your Tongue"

Author: Deirdre Patterson

Patterson Publishing Group

Tongue Action

Table of Contents

Introduction

An affirmation is the confirmation or ratification of the truth. It is a statement that is declared to be true. It's the validity or decision of a prior judgment. It is designed to change your mind and position you for the blessings the Lord have promised you.

In this book you will find forty affirmations inspired by Holy Spirit that will bless your life. Now be truthful with yourself and look around you. What you see around you is a result of your tongue action. Now that the word affirmation has been defined you are clear on what an affirmation is. They are designed to change your thoughts and your cause your faith to increase.

When you begin to recite them, there will be a shift in the atmosphere and things will begin to happen according to your faith. Reciting these affirmations will cause things in your life come into spiritual alignment. I can attest to this. When the Lord began to deal with me concerning my words and the power our words have, things in my life began to change when I lined my mouth and my thoughts with the word of God.

The word says in *Proverbs 18:21*, **Death and life are in the power of the tongue and they that love it shall eat the fruit thereof.** What the Lord revealed to me is that when we realize that the power is in our words, whether good or bad, whatever we love speaking we will eat the fruit thereof. When we start to declare and speak life in the atmosphere, to our situations, our families, and those around us we will experience change, manifestation of blessings, and increased faith. Where change is needed speak affirmations and the word of God over your life and command change.

As a believer of the word of God and one that is in right relationship with the Father in heaven, the declaration you will make by reciting these affirmations will transform, reconstruct, and empower you mentally and spiritually to push forward in the things of God. These affirmations were created to shift atmospheres, mindsets, and also to activate your faith.

The Holy Spirit instructed me to write forty affirmations for each year of my life. In the Hebrew 40 is derived from the letter "mem" (water, flowing, coming from). 40 is the number of trial or probation.

When viewed as a time cycle, we discovered that the children of Israel spent 40 years being tested in the wilderness; Jesus spent 40 days in the wilderness being tempted by the devil. Yes, these have a negative connotation however in the positive sense, forty (i.e., mem) speaks of Israel crossing the Jordan River (water) after 40 years in the wilderness.

This depiction is that Israel came from the wilderness and flowed into the Promised Land. As you read these affirmation your Egypt (bondage, hindrance) will loose it's strong holds and your deliverance into Canaan will be yours.

There will be seasons in your life that the affirmations that you have chosen to recite will shift your way of thinking, increase your faith and give you that extra push needed to find and fulfill your destiny in Christ Jesus.

Recite the affirmations needed daily. My prayer is that they inspire you, change your way of thinking, bring you to manifested promises of the Lord, and activate your God-given ability to walk in power and authority. There are challenges where the results will manifest blessings that the Lord has in store for those that believe.

The power of life and death are in your tongue. (*Proverbs 18:21*) You have the power to create an atmosphere conducive for manifestation of God's promises and to create divine intervention and creativity in your life. Don't allow what you see to be a determining factor of your outcome.

As you proceed with your reading, my prayer is that you are blessed by the contents of this reading and that the manifested blessings of the Lord will overtake you in Jesus name.

Dedication

I'd like to dedicate this, my first book, to my awesome daughter CiJi.

Thank you for believing in me and the vision that the Lord has blessed me with. May the Lord richly bless you and keep you in Jesus name.

Chapter 1

Speak Life

Have you ever had the feeling that everyone around you is being blessed except you? Have you ever felt like that you try to dot every "I" and cross every "T", serve the Lord to the best of your ability? Do often wonder when it is going to be my turn to be blessed and happy? Well if these are questions that you have been asking yourself then this is the book for you.

In this reading, you will discover the power that your tongue possesses. The bible declares that there is the power of life and death in the tongues and whatever we speak is what will be produced. So I remember in prayer my time talking to the Lord and asking those questions concerning me, my family, my finances and about every area of my life. This is what the Lord spoke to me. He said, "You have the keys to my kingdom and you have yet to utilize them. The reason you have not gained access to what is rightfully yours is because you have yet to understand how my kingdom works.

My kingdom in which you are in pursuit of is already in you. My glory, my spirit, my authority and power is already in YOU." Then the Lord began to teach me about affirming the word of God and speaking it into the atmosphere. He also told me that once I began doing this everyday, there would be a shift in my life. As a result of verbalizing the word of God into the air daily, mindset shifted. My faith increased, the negative thoughts left that plagued me left, my finances changed, some relationships were restored (marriage and ministry), and my gifts began to make room for me.

You will be given the tools needed to shift some things in your life. This book is to give you a foundation on how to recite affirmations but feel free to create your own. You can create affirmations to declare healing (mind, body, spirit), financial, family, job, or anything needing change or improvement in your life.

This book contains 40 affirmations to help jumpstart you in some life changing events. Recite each affirmation 10 times daily. Get a journal and record the progress in your life and the things around you. After reciting the affirmation, seal it with praise. That is how we tell the Lord that we trust Him; we believe His word and stand with great expectation of a shift for the better. Glory to God! I'm excited for you and what about to happen in your life.

Remember it is very important that you speak life in this season. Don't allow what you see to deter your faith. It's not what it looks like. We must understand the enemy plays mind games but the word tells us in *Isaiah 54:17* that ***"No weapon formed against you shall prosper, and every tongue which rises against you in judgment you shall***

condemn. This is the heritage of the servants of the Lord, and their righteousness is from Me, says the Lord." See, even in this it leads us right back to the tongue, that little powerful muscle. It doesn't weigh much but it's powerful enough to make you or break you.

So during the next 30 days let's speak life over our circumstances and counteract these weapons with speaking life through God's word and these declarations over our lives.

Day 1

I declare that through God, the battle is already won. 1Samuel 17:47

I declare that my God is preserving what he has ordained for me and He will lead me into it. Malachi 3:11; Joshua 1:16; Psalms 140:4; Ephesians 2:10

I declare that we have won the victory! 1Corinthians 15:57-58

I believe God has sent His Word and it will not return void. Isaiah 55:11

I declare that God has anointed me to so His will. Hebrews 13:21

I declare that God has given us Divine Healing and Divine Life. Matthew 8:2-3; Isaiah 53:5

I expect God's mercy and grace on me today. Lamentations 3:22-23

I expect God's favor and blessings on me today. Psalms 5:12; Jeremiah 29:11

I will live and not die, and declare the works of the Lord. Psalms 118:17

I believe God has given me His abundant life. John 10:10

Day 2

I declare today a day of productivity, strength, and consistency.

I will love my enemies, pray for them and others. (Matthew 5:44)

I will give thanks in all things for this is the will of God concerning me in Christ Jesus. (1 Thessalonians 5:18)

I shall walk in integrity and character. I am a doer of God's word.

Not just a hearer. (James 1:22-23)

I am walking in the blessing of God that makes one rich and adds no sorrow. (Proverbs 10:22)

I am walking in FULL prosperity.

I declare that whatever my circumstances may be I am determined to be positive, happy and blessed.

I will bless the Lord at all times and HIS praises shall continually be in my mouth. (Psalms 34:1)

Day 3

I declare today a day of worship, rest, fellowship and restoration.

I speak life to every dry place and command the blessing of the Lord.

I am who God's says I am. I am happy, healthy and blessed.

I declare that I will finish the things I start without procrastination and hesitation.

I will defeat the enemy by remaining in the will of God for my life and being obedient to God's instructions.

I will complete every assignment God has given me and keep praise in my mouth even when times are rough.

I will continue to walk in forgiveness and love as it is ordained by God that I do so.

I will remember God and keep His covenant in all things for HE has given me the power to create wealth. (Deuteronomy 8:18) In Jesus' name. Amen.

Day 4

I declare that today will be productive and prosperous.

I will use my time wisely in this next chapter of my life to establish my divine purpose in God.

I give more, pray more, more productive and watch God move.

I declare that everyone that recites these affirmations receive life changing results that will magnify the name of our Lord Jesus Christ.

I declare that today be a day of productivity, prosperity, and promise.

I'm awake with a greater expectation of life, love, and manifested promise.

I declare that I will continue to walk in love, life and happiness.

I speak to my atmosphere and declare that I shall live and not die and declare the works of the Lord. Lord I thank you!

I declare that today is a day of blessings and kingdom manifestation in my walk, talk, and lifestyle.

I command God's blessing that makes one rich and

adds no sorrow to be upon me, my house and also those whose lives I'm assigned to impact.

I am who God says I am and I shall walk in the power and authority ordained for my life.

I declare that God's spirit be upon everywhere I go and that praise be continually on my lips. In Jesus' name. Amen

Day 5

I declare that nothing shall separate me from God's love.

I declare that I am more than a conqueror through Christ.

I am determined to walk in kingdom power and authority given to me through Jesus Christ.

I am walking in prosperity due to manifestation of the promises of God in my life.

I shall continue to speak life and watch God move for me and my family.

I declare that today will be stress free.

This is a day of thanks for life, health and strength.

I am determined to stay in a positive place and I am around positive people.

I am happy and set free by the blood of Jesus in every area of my life and I am so glad about it.

I expect miracles, signs and wonders today. I will be a blessing today.

I am a doer of God's word not just a listener.

God's word in me has made me a blessing magnet and I give HIM praise.

I declare today a day of rest, worship and recovery.

My heart is right and ready for love. God I thank you for my family, church family and friends.

I thank you for my husband/wife.

I declare to continue to love him/her like Christ loved the church. In Jesus name. Amen

Day 6

I declare that I am healed from all the disappointments, hurts, and assignments of the enemy that have tried to destroy me.

I speak to the gifts that lay dormant in me and command them to be activated in the name of Jesus.

I command creativity and productivity to take action.

I will walk in God's covenant and I will remember God for HE has given me the power to get wealth.

I command prosperity to overtake me and my family.

I declare thanksgiving in every aspect of my life.

I declare to speak those things that be not as though they were.

My praise will be continual.

I will seek God in every aspect of my life daily.

Day 7

I declare that today is a day of thanksgiving for my life, health and strength.

I am determined to be all that God has called me to be in mind, body and spirit.

I declare that the things from my past will not plague me but I will use those things to enhance my future.

I am stronger, I walk in wisdom, and I am anointed for this journey. I am more than a conqueror.

I can have what I say.

I am in position and preparing myself for destiny and the fulfilling of my kingdom agenda.

I declare that every promise from God spoken over my life will manifest quickly.

I declare that every one of my needs will be met in Jesus' name.

My household is blessed, my child/children are blessed, and blessed people surround me.

I say yes Lord to your will for my life and I am determined to walk in the fullness of Joy.

I am fearfully and wonderfully made in the image of God.

I walk and speak in the confidence of God. Because I know my worth now others will.

I declare that everyone I come in contact with be blessed by the presence of God in my life.

I shall live, laugh and enjoy life. In Jesus' name. Amen.

Day 8

I declare today to let the mind of Christ be in me, which is also in Christ Jesus. (Philippians 2:5).

I am kept in perfect peace because my mind is stayed in Jesus. (Isaiah 26:3)

I have peace mentally in every area of my life.

I declare today and forever that whatever is true,

whatever is honest, whatever is just,

whatever is pure, whatever is lovely,

and whatever is of good report;

if there be any virtue and of there be any praise,

I WILL think about these things. (Philippians 4:8)

Day 9

I declare today that God has not given me a spirit of fear but

He has give me power, love and a sound mind. (2Timothy 1:7)

I declare to read God's word daily to renew my mind.

I declare to speak God's word to change my circumstances,

which first begins in my thoughts.

The mind of Jesus Christ is also in me.

I realize that my thoughts turn into actions,

and my actions bring manifestation.

I am whole in EVERY area of my life.

So I declare to let God's word to work on my behalf, In Jesus' name.

Day 10

I declare and decree that today be a day of manifestation.

I command the blessing that makes one rich and adds no sorrow to be upon me.

I am the righteousness of God and I am walking in FULL manifestation of HIS promises for my life.

I declare that God's anointing on my life be infectious, contagious, and that everyone that encounters it be changed into the image of God.

I speak these words because I know who I am and whose I am.

I declare today that the thoughts of my past will not plague me any longer.

The hurt from family and "so-called" friends will no longer effect me.

I am walking in the love of Jesus Christ in every area of my life because kingdom WILL NOT manifest where there is no love.

I am determined to be all that GOD has called me to be and to walk in purpose and fulfillment.

I declare today a day of rejoicing, productivity, and righteousness.

I thank you LORD it's Friday. In Jesus' name. Amen.

Day 11

I am happy, healthy, blessed and highly favored.

I am a blessing magnet and I can have what I say.

My mind is free from clutter and the worries that life have to offer.

I am fearfully and wonderfully made in the image on God.

I declare increase in knowledge, wisdom, finances, and most of all my relationship with God.

I do NOT embrace religion but relationship with Jesus Christ.

I am a believer of God's word and walk in total obedience in what it instructs me to do.

I AM impacting the places that GOD has sent me.

I AM a good thing and a blessing.

Day 12

Today I speak life and blessings over my family, my friends and myself.

I speak deliverance and that GOD have mercy over my enemies.

I declare that the bondage be removed from their lives and that they walk in total agreement with the things of God including me.

I am who God says I am. I am blessed and highly favored.

I am the righteousness of God.

I know that when the enemy comes in like a flood that God will lift up a standard against him.

The standard is peace, love, and security.

I refuse to settle for less and with God I declare the best is yet to come.

I speak deliverance and healing over my family and me in Jesus' name! Amen.

Day 13

I declare today to be the best day of my life.

I will use the breath God has given me to spread the word of HIS love for me.

I declare that I seek first the kingdom of God and HIS righteousness.

I am the righteousness of God.

I command my mind, my heart, my life to line up with God's word.

I am happy, I am healthy and I am FREE from the bondage of the enemy!!

I am destined for greatness.

I am ordained so therefore God will maintain every aspect of my life.

I am anointed to make a difference in someone's life.

I know the promises of God are yes and amen and I declare this day to walk in it fully.

I cancel every negative thought and I am determined to be a light in this dark world.

I declare that today will be a great day because God made it and I was able to see it.

I speak life to every gift that is lying dormant in me and I command it to live and not die.

I am thankful that this time I won't get left behind.

I declare that Christ Jesus will supply every need in my life according to God's riches in glory.

I declare that my life will bless someone today.

I declare and decree that God is preparing a table before me in the presence of my enemies and I will remain humble so that God will exalt me.

In Jesus' name amen!

Day 14

I thank the Lord for waking me up this morning in my right mind because it is stayed on Jesus!

Therefore I am in peace.

I declare today that I will go into the house of worship not just sitting waiting for the choir or the praise team to motivate me but to enter into worship because I'm in love with the Lord.

I declare that every broken place in my life will be fixed in Jesus' name.

I declare and decree that blessings be upon everyone that recite this affirmation and whose faith is increased as a result of belief.

I am a money magnet and will use it to increase God's kingdom.

I declare that I will walk in forgiveness and love in Jesus' name. Amen

Day 15

I declare today Fantastic Friday. Fantastic things will happen today.

I know that the power of life and death is in my tongue and I speak blessings over others today and myself.

I declare that God has created me to be a blessing to others.

I am happy, healthy, and heaven bound.

I am faithful over everything that God has given me.

As long as there is breath in my body I will give God all of me.

I will NOT lower my standards.

I will seek Gods kingdom first and everything will be added. In Jesus' name! Amen.

Day 16

Declare today to be ordained by God because HE allowed me to see it.

I am blessed in the city.

I am blessed in the field.

I am blessed in every area of my life.

I speak with the authority given to me by Christ to every dead place and I command them to live and NOT die and declare the works of the Lord.

I speak to my finances, Money "COME to me NOW" and I thank you Lord for manifestation.

I AM a faithful and wise steward over all that God has given me and what's to come so that increase will come to me, my family, and in my ministry.

Declare today is productive and blessed.

I declare that someone will get to know you cause my life is lined up in you. In Jesus' name! Amen.

Day 17

I declare today is a productive day.

I will complete tasks that have been held up.

I declare that I am in my right mind, the mind of Christ.

I am who God's says I am.

I will be effective in my ministry, family, and on my job.

I will do what God tells me to do.

For I know that obedience is better than sacrifice.

I remain humble so that God will exalt me.

I will expect the impossible to become possible in my life starting NOW.

I declare that from this day forward I will walk to carry out my kingdom agenda with a kingdom mindset, kingdom conversation, and a kingdom outcome. In Jesus' name. Amen!!!

Day 18

I declare today that I will have an encounter with the Lord that will set me free from every bondage in my life.

I will be patient and let God work things out for me.

I will celebrate God even in the midst of adverse times with NO MORE STRUGGLE.

I declare that I am happy, healthy, and ready for love, God's way.

I shall continue to live and not die and declare God's works.

I am more than a conqueror.

I am a doer of God's word not just a hearer.

I COMMAND money to come to ME from the north, south, east, west and that I am a faithful and wise steward over EVERYTHING that GOD puts in my hands.

I declare that everyone that I come in contact with me will experience GOD in an awesome way. In Jesus' name. Amen

Day 19

I declare today that I will no longer waste time cause it is a sin.

I am chasing after the kingdom of GOD in HOT pursuit of kingdom things.

Because I choose to be obedient to God's word, I know that HE will with hold nothing from me.

I have the power to speak things into existence and I exercise my authority TODAY.

I thank you Lord for my job, family, friends, husband/wife, and EVERYTHING I need and desire that is in YOUR will for my life. In Jesus' name!!! Amen.

Day 20

I declare today o be a day of worship, thanksgiving, praise, happiness.

I am blessed and highly favored. I am who GOD says I am.

I am debt free, motivated, focused and my mind is made up NOT to compromise with the enemy.

I forgive my enemies and I pray for them. I release unforgiveness, hurt, and misunderstanding from my heart in Jesus' name amen.

Day 21

I declare today that I will be surrounded by love, laughter, and peace.

The peace of God that will surpass my understanding and that will rest in my hart and in my mind.

I declare that I will continue to rejoice and be glad in the today because the LORD made it.

I command my finances, my mind, and my life to line up with the word of God.

I declare and decree that I prosper and be in GOOD health even as my soul prospers.

Day 22

I am happy, healthy, and I shall live and not die and declare God's work in the land of the living.

I walk in love and am a giver of love.

I am the head and not the tail I am above and not beneath.

I am a doer of God's word not just a hearer.

I am affirming God's word because I know that death and life is in my tongue.

I choose to speak life. My family and friends are blessed. I thank you LORD!

Day 23

I declare this day a day of Thanksgiving.

I thank you Lord for life, health and strength.

I declare that my family is well and that your favor is in our lives.

I declare that my steps are ordered by you, Lord and

That you are directing my path.

I will rejoice in this day that the Lord has made.

I declare that God will withhold NO good thing from me cause I am obedient to HIS word.

I declare happiness, great health, and prosperity.

In Jesus' name amen.

Day 24

Lord, I thank you for waking me up this morning.

I am thankful for all that you are doing for me, my family and my community.

I declare that this life was given to me to make a difference and not just be concerned with myself.

I am who God says I am. I am the head and NOT the tail. I am above and not beneath.

I am the lender and not the borrower. I am financially free. All of my needs are supplied.

Because I live for you LORD my life is changing for the better.

I speak prosperity, I think prosperity and therefore I am prosperous.

I declare that this is the day that the Lord had made and I will rejoice and be glad in it. Hallelujah!

Day 25

Lord I thank you for waking me upset this.

I am healthy, happy, and prosperous.

I am the righteous of God.

I am justified, completely forgiven and made righteous (Romans5:1)

I have the mind of Christ (Philippians 2:5)

I can do all things in Christ (Philippians 4:13)

I am secure in the Lord (Romans 8:38-39)

The Lord is my refuge (Psalm 91:9-10)

I am determined to follow Christ in every aspect of my life.

I declare God's favor, humility and blessing upon me, my family, and my

lineage.

I declare all curses have been broken in Jesus' name!!!! Amen!

Day 26

Thank you Lord for allowing me to see this day that you have made.

I will rejoice and be glad in it.

I declare today that I am one of God's living stones and I am being built up as a spiritual house. (1Peter 2:5)

I am Part of a chosen race, a royal priesthood, a holy nation. (1Peter 2:9-10)

I am the enemy of the devil (1 Peter 5:8) I am justified, completely forgiven and made righteous. (Romans 5:1)

I am dead with Christ and dead to the power of sin's rule over my life. (Romans 6:1-6)

I am given the Holy spirit as a pledge, a guarantee of my inheritance. (Ephesians 1:13-14)

These words I declare over me, my family, my friends, and me enemies. I declare that God's blessings on me today.

I declare that my life is not my own and however GOD sees fit to use me today I am willing.

I walk in DIVINE favor in Jesus' name. HALLELUJAH!

Day 27

It is written in Psalms 34:19 that the afflictions of the righteous are many, but YOU will deliver us from them all.

Lord, your word will strengthen my weak hands and strengthen my feeble knees. (Job 4:3-4)

You Lord will heal all my sickness and diseases. (Matthew 4:23-24)

I listen to the voice of the Lord and do what is right in HIS eyes and HE heals me. (Exodus 15:26)

The Lord is merciful to my weaknesses and HE heals me (Psalms 6:22)

I declare today that prosperity upon me and house.

I declare that I am content in the place that God has set me.

I declare that my attitude of gratitude will increase daily. In Jesus' name!

Day 28

I declare that God forgives all my iniquities, and heals all my diseases. (Proverbs 103:3)

Lord, your word says that if I cry out to YOU, YOU will heal me. (Psalms 30:2)

Lord, it is written in YOUR word that YOU will take away from me all my sickness. (Deuteronomy 7:15)

I am a new creation in God (2 Corinthians 5:17)

I am content with the Lord (Philippians 4:11)

I am secure in the Lord (Romans 8:38-39)

I am free in YOU Lord! (Romans 6:18)

I am happy. I declare that today will be a great, productive, and blessed day.

I command my mind, my words, lifestyle, my finances, my family, and my friends to line up with your word and to walk in divine destiny and favor that ONLY comes from you. In Jesus' name. AMEN!!!

Day 29

Deuteronomy 11:8-16

I declare that as I keep all the Lord's commandments I will be strong, and I will go and possess the land.

The shall prolong my days in the land, which the Lord swore to my fathers and their seed, the land that flow with milk and honey.

I will possess the land. This land is not like Egypt or like any bondage I came out of, but the land is a land of prosperity, a land with hills, valleys, and rain from heaven.

This is a land that the Lord thy God cares for and has given me the power to possess it.

The eyes of the Lord are always upon it so therefore I'm protected.

From the beginning of the year until the end of the year the Lord will give provision.

I declare that it shall come to pass if I obey God's commandments to love Him with all my heart and all of my soul.

I declare that God will give me rain in due season.

The former rain and the latter rain, I may gather the

increase in my businesses, ministry, properties, and everything I'm destined to possess.

God is sending prosperity and I receive it in Jesus' name.

Day 30

I declare that through God, the battle is already won. (1 Samuel 17:47)

I declare that my God is preserving what has ordained for me and He will lead me into.

I declare that we have won the victory. (1 Corinthians 15:57-58)

I believe God has sent His Word and it will not return void. (Isaiah 55:11)

I declare that God has anointed us to do His will. (Hebrews 13:21)

I cast down every vain imagination and every high thing that exalts itself against the knowledge of God, and bring every thought captive to the obedience of the Lord Jesus Christ.

Chapter 2

Welcome to the Overflow

In this chapter are some additional affirmations to jumpstart your life. These are 10 affirmations that were inspired by the Holy Spirit to help you realize who you are and whose you are. You are a kingdom citizen. Due to your citizenship their laws, statues, accesses granted to you because of it.

Affirmation 31

Death and life is in the power of the tongue and they that indulge in it shall eat the fruit there of. (Proverbs 18:21)

So today I choose to speak life over every area of my life.

I speak life to my mind.

I speak life to my body.

I speak life to my spirit man.

I command every area of my life to come in alignment with God's word.

My words and my thought will line up with God's word.

I also speak your word over my finances. 3 John 1:2 says Beloved, I wish above all thing that thou may prosper and be in good health even as thy soul prospers.

Your word also declares in Mark11:23 and these are they which sown on good ground; such as hear the word and receive it, and bring forth fruit, some thirty fold, sixty fold and some a hundred fold.

So Lord I receive your word and now I expect my

increase. In Jesus' name. Amen.

Affirmation 32

God's word tells me that if I listen to His voice and follow his instructions, He will set me high above the nations.

All these things shall come upon me if I heed the voice of the Lord.

I declare that I am obedient to God's voice.

I am blessed in the city and in the field.

I am blessed in the fruit of my body.

I am healed.

I am blessed in the fruit of the ground.

I am good ground.

I am blessed in the fruit of my beasts, cattle and flock.

I am blessed in my basket and the works of my hands are increased.

I am blessed when I come in and when I go out.

 The Lord shall cause my enemies who rise up against me to be defeated before my face.

They shall come out against me one way and flee seven ways.

The Lord shall command the blessing upon me in the land that He shall give me.

The has established me as one of His people and has sworn to me as long as I keep His commandments and walk in His word.

According to His holy word, all people shall call me by the name and in the presence of the Lord and shall be afraid of me.

The Lord shall make me to have a surplus of prosperity, through the fruits of my body, of my livestock, of my ground, in the land that the Lord swore unto my forefathers to give me.

I declare that I shall have what I say cause I WILL speak life in Jesus name.

Amen. The Lord shall open up to me Hid good treasury, the heavens, to give the rain on my land in it's season and to bless all the works of my hands.

I shall lend to many nations and NOT borrow.

The Lord has made me the head and not the tail.

I am above only and not beneath.

All this will be and remain upon me as I am obedient to the Lord, In Jesus' name Amen. (Deuteronomy 28:1-14)

Affirmation 33

I declare today that I will not be conformed to this world,

 but be changed by the entire renewal of my mind, a new way of thinking, new attitude that lines up with God's will for my life,

so that I may prove to myself that this is a good and acceptable will of God. (Roman 12:2)

I declare to strip myself of old thoughts, old actions, and an old nature.

I will put on a new mindset, new attitude and new faith through God's word. (Ephesians 4:22)

I am washed, sanctified, and justified in the name of the Lord Jesus Christ and by the blood of the Lamb.

My body is a temple of the Holy Spirit, who is in me, whom I have received from God.

I am not my own.

I was bought with a price.

I desire to walk in the spirit and not fulfill the lust of the flesh.

Affirmation 34

I declare today to let the mind of Christ be in me, which is also in Christ Jesus. (Philippians 2:5).

I am kept in perfect peace because my mind is stayed in Jesus. (Isaiah 26:3) I have peace mentally and in every area of my life.

I declare today and forever that I will not fret because of evil doers neither will I be envious against workers of iniquity. (Psalms 37:1)

I will trust in the Lord and do good.

I shall live in the land and I shall be fed.

I will delight myself in the Lord and the Lord shall give me the desires of my heart. (Psalms 37:3-4)

Affirmation 35

I declare today that God has not given me a spirit of fear but He has give me power, love and a sound mind. (2Timothy 1:7)

I declare to read God's word daily to renew my mind.

I declare to speak God's word to change my circumstances, which first begins in my thoughts.

I realize that my thoughts turn into actions, and my actions bring manifestation.

I yield no ground to Satan.

I take back all that I have ever surrendered to him in the past and acknowledge that the Jesus is the Lord of all of my life.

So I declare to let God's word to work on my behalf, In Jesus' name.

Affirmation 36

I declare that I will continue to walk in love, life and happiness.

I speak to my atmosphere and declare that I shall live and not die and declare the works of the Lord.

Lord I thank you!

I declare that today is a day of blessings and kingdom manifestation in my walk, talk, and lifestyle.

I command God's blessing that makes one rich and adds no sorrow to be upon me, my house and those I'm assigned to impact.

I am who God says I am and I shall walk in the power and authority ordained for my life.

I declare that God's spirit be upon everywhere I go and that praise be continually on my lips.

In Jesus' name. Amen

Affirmation 38

I declare that I am more than a conqueror.

I am healed, delivered and set free from the bondage.

I am free from sickness and disease.

Sickness is not welcome here.

Disease is not welcome.

I am whole.

The Holy Spirit fills every void in my life.

The Lord guides me.

The Lord protects.

He shows the unseen.

I thank you Lord for freedom, wholeness, and prosperity.

In Jesus' name. Amen.

Affirmation 39

I declare that today the pain of rejection is no longer apart of my life.

I cast the bitterness, strife, anger, rejection, and resentment of past relationships back to the pit of hell where it belongs.

I declare freedom in the name of Jesus.

I declare that I am wrapped in God's love and HIS presence and that is where I shall remain.

Lord I declare today that I receive your anointing which is your presence that destroys every yoke of bondage that tries to attack me.

Isaiah 53:5 says that you oh Lord have taken the striped that I might be healed and for this Lord I thank you.

Affirmation 40

I declare today that I am standing on the word of God.

In the name of Jesus I bind every one of Satan's evil spirits, occult spirits, demonic forces, satanic powers, principalities, attributes, clusters, endowments, and satanic thrones, darkness positions of authority, satanic rankings, and offices.

I bind all princes of darkness, jurisdictional reigns, territorial government and the activities of the air in which they govern.

I cast all out of it out of my spirit, mind, body and everyone I am in contact with in the name of Jesus.

The word says I can call on the name of Jesus and I shall be delivered.

Today I declare my deliverance in the name of Jesus.

So today I call on you Jesus to deliverance from all hindrances and I decree and declare my freedom in Christ in Jesus' matchless name!

After reciting these affirmations over yourself, over your family, and in the atmosphere, stop; and give the Lord praise. Your praise solidifies that you believe the words that you've just spoken and that you are now patiently waiting for the Lord to move on your behalf.

There is a scripture that my husband and I recite 10'xs daily is Psalm 115:14. It says the Lord shall increase you more and more, you and your family. We personalized this scripture. Our declaration is "The Lord shall increase me more and more; me and my family.

Before we started to recite this scripture, I lost my job. There was so much that my family needed. My husband had lost his job months prior and now mine. During our devotion, the Lord reminded of this scripture that I used to affirm and for some reason I had stopped. So after sharing with my husband what the Lord had spoken to me, we began that day to recite Psalms 115:14 10 times daily.

The next day my husband got a phone calls and now his security business has been restored. His income is more than enough. Manifested blessings began to overtake our household. As for me, my husband came to me and told me that if I wanted to stay home and work on some projects that the Lord had given me, that he was bringing in enough income for me to do so.

At first I was reluctant because I was thinking if we had

two incomes we could do a lot more.

The next day in my prayer time, the Lord spoke to me and said listen to your husband and finish the assignments that I've given you. My response was, "yes Lord".

There was a struggle, because I was used to being independent and earning my own pay. As the days past, the enemy began to put thoughts in my head to seek employment and I did. I became restless. Then the Lord asked me if I trusted Him. I put the computer down and began to repent for allowing doubt to come in. I started praying and repenting again to the Lord for not trusting Him fully. I had to remember faith and doubt don't mix. So I began to recite Psalms 115:14 again and again with my husband. The next day, I receive a phone call where someone was looking for a grant writer and a business consultant. Increase manifested again. Let's just say that I was hired and my first check was more than I made in a month on my last job. The Lord has brought so much increase to our house that we don't have room enough to receive.

As a kingdom citizen, the Holy Spirit dwells inside of you, and has given you an all access granted pass to speak things that don't exist as though they are in existence. (Romans 4:17) For instance in the kingdom, we don't speak that we're going to be healed.

Kingdom language is that YOU ARE HEALED.

So begin to line up your thoughts, your words and your actions with God's word and see the results.

About the Author

Apostle Deirdre Patterson is a mother, psalmist, author, conference speaker, Business development consultant, grant writer, and teacher. She has been in ministry since July 1996 and is passionate about spreading the gospel of Jesus Christ, the gospel of the kingdom and making a difference in the lives of those she's been sent to.

She is a Doctor of Christian Education from ABG Alliance and Seminary in Charlotte, NC. She received her undergraduate degree in Mass Communications from Fayetteville State University.

She is the founder of Empowered for Change Deliverance Churches International

To book Deirdre, please contact us at e4c2005@gmail.com

My Daily Fasting and Praying Journal: Day 1

My Daily Fasting and Praying Journal: Day 2

_____

_____

_____

_____

_____

_____

_____

_____

_____

_____

_____

_____

_____

_____

_____

_____

_____

_____

_____

_____

_____

_____

_____

_____

_____

My Daily Fasting and Praying Journal: Day 3

_____

_____

_____

_____

_____

_____

_____

_____

_____

_____

_____

_____

_____

_____

_____

_____

_____

_____

_____

_____

_____

_____

_____

_____

_____

My Daily Fasting and Praying Journal: Day 4

My Daily Fasting and Praying Journal: Day 5

_____

_____

_____

_____

_____

_____

_____

_____

_____

_____

_____

_____

_____

_____

_____

_____

_____

_____

_____

_____

_____

_____

_____

_____

_____

_____

My Daily Fasting and Praying Journal: Day 6

_____

_____

_____

_____

_____

_____

_____

_____

_____

_____

_____

_____

_____

_____

_____

_____

_____

_____

_____

_____

_____

_____

_____

_____

_____

My Daily Fasting and Praying Journal: Day 7

_____

_____

_____

_____

_____

_____

_____

_____

_____

_____

_____

_____

_____

_____

_____

_____

_____

_____

_____

_____

_____

_____

_____

_____

My Daily Fasting and Praying Journal: Day 8

My Daily Fasting and Praying Journal: Day 9

_____

_____

_____

_____

_____

_____

_____

_____

_____

_____

_____

_____

_____

_____

_____

_____

_____

_____

_____

_____

_____

_____

_____

_____

_____

_____

_____

My Daily Fasting and Praying Journal: Day 10

_____

_____

_____

_____

_____

_____

_____

_____

_____

_____

_____

_____

_____

_____

_____

_____

_____

_____

_____

_____

_____

_____

_____

_____

_____

_____

_____

_____

My Daily Fasting and Praying Journal: Day 11

My Daily Fasting and Praying Journal: Day 12

_____

_____

_____

_____

_____

_____

_____

_____

_____

_____

_____

_____

_____

_____

_____

_____

_____

_____

_____

_____

_____

_____

_____

_____

_____

_____

My Daily Fasting and Praying Journal: Day 13

My Daily Fasting and Praying Journal: Day 14

My Daily Fasting and Praying Journal: Day 15

_____

_____

_____

_____

_____

_____

_____

_____

_____

_____

_____

_____

_____

_____

_____

_____

_____

_____

_____

_____

_____

_____

_____

_____

_____

_____

_____

_____

_____

My Daily Fasting and Praying Journal: Day 16

_____
_____
_____
_____
_____
_____
_____
_____
_____
_____
_____
_____
_____
_____
_____
_____
_____
_____
_____
_____
_____
_____
_____
_____
_____

My Daily Fasting and Praying Journal: Day 17

_____

_____

_____

_____

_____

_____

_____

_____

_____

_____

_____

_____

_____

_____

_____

_____

_____

_____

_____

_____

_____

_____

_____

_____

_____

_____

_____

My Daily Fasting and Praying Journal: Day 18

_____

_____

_____

_____

_____

_____

_____

_____

_____

_____

_____

_____

_____

_____

_____

_____

_____

_____

_____

_____

_____

_____

_____

My Daily Fasting and Praying Journal: Day 19

_____

_____

_____

_____

_____

_____

_____

_____

_____

_____

_____

_____

_____

_____

_____

_____

_____

_____

_____

_____

_____

_____

_____

_____

_____

_____

My Daily Fasting and Praying Journal: Day 20

_____
_____
_____
_____
_____
_____
_____
_____
_____
_____
_____
_____
_____
_____
_____
_____
_____
_____
_____
_____
_____
_____
_____
_____
_____

My Daily Fasting and Praying Journal: Day 21

My Daily Fasting and Praying Journal: 22

My Daily Fasting and Praying Journal: Day 23

_____

_____

_____

_____

_____

_____

_____

_____

_____

_____

_____

_____

_____

_____

_____

_____

_____

_____

_____

_____

_____

_____

_____

_____

_____

_____

_____

My Daily Fasting and Praying Journal: Day 24

My Daily Fasting and Praying Journal: Day 25

My Daily Fasting and Praying Journal: Day 26

_____

_____

_____

_____

_____

_____

_____

_____

_____

_____

_____

_____

_____

_____

_____

_____

_____

_____

_____

_____

_____

_____

_____

_____

_____

_____

_____

_____

_____

My Daily Fasting and Praying Journal: Day 27

_____

_____

_____

_____

_____

_____

_____

_____

_____

_____

_____

_____

_____

_____

_____

_____

_____

_____

_____

_____

_____

_____

_____

_____

_____

_____

_____

_____

My Daily Fasting and Praying Journal: Day 28

_____
_____
_____
_____
_____
_____
_____
_____
_____
_____
_____
_____
_____
_____
_____
_____
_____
_____
_____
_____
_____
_____
_____
_____
_____
_____
_____

My Daily Fasting and Praying Journal: Day 29

My Daily Fasting and Praying Journal: Day 30

_____

_____

_____

_____

_____

_____

_____

_____

_____

_____

_____

_____

_____

_____

_____

_____

_____

_____

_____

_____

_____

_____

_____

_____

_____

_____

_____

_____

My Daily Fasting and Praying Journal: Day 31

_____
_____
_____
_____
_____
_____
_____
_____
_____
_____
_____
_____
_____
_____
_____
_____
_____
_____
_____
_____
_____
_____
_____
_____
_____
_____

My Daily Fasting and Praying Journal: Day 32

_____

_____

_____

_____

_____

_____

_____

_____

_____

_____

_____

_____

_____

_____

_____

_____

_____

_____

_____

_____

_____

_____

_____

_____

_____

My Daily Fasting and Praying Journal: Day 33

My Daily Fasting and Praying Journal: Day 34

_____

_____

_____

_____

_____

_____

_____

_____

_____

_____

_____

_____

_____

_____

_____

_____

_____

_____

_____

_____

_____

_____

_____

_____

My Daily Fasting and Praying Journal: Day 35

_____

_____

_____

_____

_____

_____

_____

_____

_____

_____

_____

_____

_____

_____

_____

_____

_____

_____

_____

_____

_____

_____

_____

_____

My Daily Fasting and Praying Journal: Day 36

_____

_____

_____

_____

_____

_____

_____

_____

_____

_____

_____

_____

_____

_____

_____

_____

_____

_____

_____

_____

_____

_____

_____

_____

My Daily Fasting and Praying Journal: Day 37

_____

_____

_____

_____

_____

_____

_____

_____

_____

_____

_____

_____

_____

_____

_____

_____

_____

_____

_____

_____

_____

_____

_____

_____

_____

My Daily Fasting and Praying Journal: Day 38

My Daily Fasting and Praying Journal: Day 39

_____

_____

_____

_____

_____

_____

_____

_____

_____

_____

_____

_____

_____

_____

_____

_____

_____

_____

_____

_____

_____

_____

_____

_____

_____

My Daily Fasting and Praying Journal: Day 40

_____
_____
_____
_____
_____
_____
_____
_____
_____
_____
_____
_____
_____
_____
_____
_____
_____
_____
_____
_____
_____
_____
_____
_____

www.ingramcontent.com/pod-product-compliance
Lightning Source LLC
Chambersburg PA
CBHW060356050426

42449CB00009B/1761